THE P.E.O PROGRAMME

How to Overcome Your Blocks to Success

JOHN KENNY

Copyright © 2019 by John Kenny

All rights reserved. This book or any portion thereof may not be reproduced or used in any manner whatsoever without the express written permission of the publisher except for the use of brief quotations in a book review.

Printed in the United Kingdom
First Printing, 2019

ISBN 978-1-9993742-0-4 (Print)
ISBN 978-1-9993742-1-1 (eBook)

John Kenny
Hertford Heath
Hertford
SG13 7PL

www.johnkennycoaching.com

People who know and accept themselves
do not need to seek validation from
outside opinion or the attainment of goals.

They are truly at peace with themselves
and the world around them.

They are not fazed by criticism,
or seeking praise, but are fuelled
by their own happiness and self-love.

They choose how they live their lives
and how successful they are going to
allow themselves to be.

John Kenny

I dedicate this book to Mr John Platt who left this life far too early.

I am forever grateful for your time, energy, support, encouragement, belief and friendship.

Testimonial

This is the type of book that you don't want to put down. You feel as though John is talking directly to "You".

If you want to really understand yourself and understand why you feel and react to " those situations"in your life, then this book is an absolute must to personally develop yourself to a positive and peaceful place.

Des O'Connor
Award winning entrepreneur, International Speaker and Founder of Women in Business and Dating and Relationship Conferences.

Contents

Prologue — 7

One: To be Seen or Not to be Seen: Which is Safer? — 9

Two: My Same Old Story — 15

Three: The Power of a Belief — 23

Four: Good Luck Changing Others — 29

Five: Developing Relationships — 37

Six: Developing My Personality — 45

Seven: So, What Changed? — 55

Eight: The P.E.O.P.L.E Programme – Why? — 61

Nine: The First P of The P.E.O.P.L.E. Programme — 65

Ten: The First E of The P.E.O.P.L.E. Programme — 71

Eleven: The O of The P.E.O.P.L.E. Programme — 75

Twelve: The Second P of The P.E.O.P.L.E. Programme   ***81***

Thirteen: The L of The P.E.O.P.L.E. Programme   ***89***

Fourteen: The Second E of The P.E.O.P.L.E. Programme   ***95***

Fifteen: Not Just Relationships   ***103***

Epilogue   ***107***

Prologue

The date doesn't really matter, as this could be at any time in someone's life. This just happens to be about me and my childhood.

Picture if you will a small boy, around five years of age, sitting at a dining room table with his crayons and paper. The radio is playing in the background, and the smell of Sunday lunch wafts from the kitchen.

"Mummy, look, I have done you a drawing."

"Not now John, I am making lunch."

"But Mummy, I have done it for you, it's a tree!"

"I said, not now, go and play with your brother and leave me to cook."

"But you asked me to draw you something!"

"Did I? Oh well, I don't have time to look, I will look later."

But I knew, even at this age, that later would never come.

"Go and play with your brother and let me get on."

"But he will hit me again if I want to play; he always has to win."

"Well don't wind him up then, and you know that he needs to win everything, so just let him."

I think to myself, "Why should I let him win; why can't I win for a change?"

It is then I hear the front door closing and decide that it is time for me to head to my room and play by myself. It is better that way, not having to lose to my brother without fear of being punched and I don't want to hear the arguments that will follow Dad's arrival and definitely don't want to get in his way. Playing by myself, keeping my own company is the best way to be.

Chapter One
To be Seen or Not to be Seen: Which is Safer?

I must have been seven or eight years of age when I ran away from home – I don't know if it was the first time, but definitely wasn't the last. I did this occasionally and never went very far but could be gone for hours. Anyway, this one occasion stands out as my parents still talk about this now with great amusement at the shock on my mum's face. I don't recall where I had been, but usually I would go to a block of flats about a mile away and sit on the benches there in the gardens and just wait. Occasionally someone would ask why I was there, and I would say I am just waiting for my parents, which was the truth I guess. I was waiting for them to come and find me.

It had got dark, so I headed home and remember climbing over our neighbours' fence to get into our back garden and come in the back door. I am not sure if I was trying to sneak in due to the lateness of the hour, as I don't remember if I tried the front door bell for someone to let me in. It was obviously very late as the back door was locked; remember that I was only seven or eight years old.

I don't know what my dad was doing at the time, some kind of building work as he had always been in to DIY, but he had left his ladders out in the garden propped up against the back of the house, going up to the roof. The window to the bedroom that I shared with my brother was open, so I thought I would just climb up and get in that way. When I reached the window however, as I looked in, to my surprise I saw my mum and my (soon to be) stepmother reading my brother a bedtime story, so I couldn't climb in undetected after all but had to knock on the window to be let in downstairs.

Now as a child this didn't seem to strike me as odd; well, I don't think it did, but I am sure that somewhere in my young mind I must have been thinking: "It is late enough to be dark, the back door is locked, my brother is in bed having a story read to him and no one has even thought about where I might be – this can't be right!"

Now the reason this story is still recited by my family is for amusement: the knocking on my bedroom window and then the terrified look on my mum's face – her shock and then screaming and shouting at me for scaring everyone: being told to get down from the ladder and ready for bed. What is not funny and is completely overlooked when reciting this story is that I am a young child, out late by myself, in the dark, and I had not been seen for hours, obviously had missed my dinner, and my brother is all tucked up in bed! And I haven't been missed!

What did I used to run away for? Well, looking back now, I had no idea at the time. It actually made no difference to my situation; if anything, it just made me feel worse. Imagine running away from home at that age, being gone for several hours, and no one even noticing.

I now know that it was all about getting some attention. I wanted someone to come and find me, to be upset I wasn't there, to miss me. I don't remember getting positive attention as a child, all of my memories are of times when I was sad, upset, scared, being picked on or ignored. Looking for attention just reinforced the fact that I didn't seem to matter to anyone or at times when I did, it was for a negative reason. Nothing I tried ever got me the positive attention that I craved, so I ended up doing negative things just to get noticed. I did like to put on a bit of a show too and remember that this would get me some attention. I had a massive cuddly toy dog, that we called Derek. I would pretend to fight him and have us both get thrown around the living room in front of my mum to entertain her. This did get me some attention, and explains why, as I got older I used to show off a bit, be silly and funny, to get attention.

My parents divorced when I was nine, my mum moved out, and my brother and I lived with my dad and stepmother. They got married the same year as my parents divorced, but I won't go in to all of that. Let us just say I was very confused about how relationships were supposed to work looking at how my parents carried out theirs. After Mum moved out, although not immediately after, I saw her for one night in the week and on Saturday afternoons.

When I was around ten or eleven years old, my mum took me to visit my grandfather and I remember being outside his house with her. I argued with her over something that I can't recall, and because I was rude to her, my grandfather slapped me as hard as he could (or it seemed like that to me) around my face and I fell to the floor – boy did that hurt! Once I picked myself up off of the floor in shock, I ran away as fast as I could, crying, and ended up in the local park. I sat there in the playground and watched some people playing football.

I remember it getting dark and I was cold, so I headed back to my grandfather's house and when I arrived I was met with another slap for running away and was made to apologise to my mum. Then I was told off that I had made her late to get me back to my dad. When anything happened where I was told off, I would always have to be the one to apologise or try and make things okay; otherwise, I was just ignored or told to stay in my room until I had.

My relationship with my brother also impacted on me in a negative way. He always had to be right and if we played games, always had to win. If I was to try and get my point across or would be winning he would lose his temper and hurt me in some way. If I was to retaliate then I would get into trouble for winding him up. It became easier over time to just let him get his own way, to avoid getting hurt or told off.

What messages did I get from all this? Well, even when I knew I hadn't done anything wrong, or I had been treated unfairly, I had to be the one to go to them in order for the relationship to be okay; I had to fit in with what others wanted in order for me to be accepted and avoid any pain.

It was only when I was playing out with the other kids in my road that I ever felt anything positive. Maybe because I was the eldest of the kids who were always out in the street, I could be in charge and get them to play the games I wanted. I used to hate it when my brother would try and join in, or some of the older kids, as they would try and take over. Again, I would be ignored or feel less important. I would then resort to heading inside dejected, go to my room and play on my own with my toys. It was my way of surviving my pain, my way of coping.

All of these experiences, and many similar, determined the way that I came to think and feel about myself. It taught me how to relate to others, and where my place was in life. When I could feel good and positive, and when I would struggle. My brain was learning how I could survive.

That's right, survive. My young brain's only job at that age was to learn how to keep me alive. How to cope with the things that were happening and for me to get through it all. My brain learnt and developed strategies in order to keep me safe, to remember what certain things felt like so that I had a way of coping when they happened again.

At the same time, as a young child, my brain waves were in the Theta range, a slower wave that all children have as it allows learning at a deeper, more profound level. I will talk a bit more about these later.

So, at this time in my life my experiences were quite literally imprinted into my brain for life. The neural pathways were set and the messages I absorbed became part of my physical existence. No wonder they were so hard to shift when I finally became aware of them.

Chapter Two
My Same Old Story

"John, do you know that Victoria likes you?"

"No, really?"

"Yes, she wants to know if you want to sit in the Wendy House with her?"

If you don't know what a Wendy House is then you have missed out! It is a little playhouse that we had in the corner of the classroom at Primary school. You could go in there and play if you were good, as all the toys were kept in there.

Wow, Victoria wants me to go into the Wendy House. I am only seven and she is eight, and she wants me to go and sit with her. After that day we would sit together during stories holding hands. A light of acceptance, someone wanting to be with me and take notice... and then she was gone!

Not a word, no warning, just gone. I later found out she had moved away, but again I felt as though I was not worth anything. She had left me without a word. The positive or 'the light appearing' that I did take from this situation is that I felt good when a girl wanted to be with me. This formed an idea within me that I could feel good with female attention and it led me to a life that was driven to get this feeling again, and again and again. I would love playing 'kiss chase' in the playground and wanted to be caught (probably like so many other children, and adults). I even remember crying once because no one was chasing me.

This kind of behaviour, needing attention, went on into my twenties. I would go out clubbing every week with my friends. I went through an angry phase at one stage, if I had gone out and not managed to get a girl's phone number. I was angry at myself for failing, but actually I was in a lot of pain, feeling unloved and unworthy of attention. It turned out that this light was not very bright at all as it led me to valuing myself externally just because of the female attention I was able to attract. If I didn't get any, I would really turn on myself.

It wasn't long after the episode with Victoria at school, so I must have been eight years old, that my mother had also left me (not me per se, but that's maybe how I saw it).

I was very angry at my mum at that time, so much so that for a while I didn't want to see her after she left; I think I was punishing her for the first nine years of our relationship. I know I thought when I was younger she preferred my brother over me. She always seemed to take his side on things, and I now know after talking to her as an adult, that it was easier for her to do this. I was easily placated and, probably because I craved love, would try not to upset her and would behave. She said my brother was very needy as a child and felt she had to take his side in order to keep him happy, otherwise his behaviour was very difficult for her to manage.

I now realise that me not seeing her was me trying to take some kind of control; to try and make myself feel important, if she would only just ask to see me. I remember my dad dropping my brother at her new place and I was in the car. As we drove away I had this longing to see her, but couldn't bring myself to go in.

This continued throughout my life in relationships with women: needing to feel wanted and special.

At the beginning of a relationship I would give 110%, be the best partner that they could ever want, but it wasn't me being genuine. I wanted to give so much to get them to accept me but was also waiting for it to be reciprocated. When it didn't arrive, I would feel resentful and withdraw emotionally.

Whenever I didn't feel loved or special enough, whenever there was an argument I would deliver this grand statement that I was leaving and would never be seen again in the hope that they would value me enough to give in or chase me. If they didn't, for a while at least I would try and make things right again, but eventually I would walk away and never go back as my protective barriers from childhood were up, and they would never go back down again.

This was the case with someone I met when I had just turned thirty, where I couldn't see past my own needs. The relationship was going really well, and we moved in together fairly quickly. I thought she would be the one at that time. Unfortunately, a series of events led her to feel depressed and shut down her emotions for a while. Immediately my barriers went up to protect myself and I was unable to let them down again as she came out the other side. For me, to let my feelings out would have been too much of a risk, in case she withdrew again.

My expectation that relationships could never be right for me, even if the issues were small or through no fault of anyone, meant that I would be off to find someone else to give to and feel special with. I was very conflicted about trying to make people happy and feeling important enough to them too.

This was my relationship pattern set. I was mostly attracted to relationships where I could give a lot at the start and it would blossom, I would feel happy and content, and so would they, to a degree. Then after a while I would get upset and annoyed because either I was not getting enough back in return, or I felt as though what I was giving wasn't enough for them or appreciated enough. Both of these made me reflect on myself as not good enough, just like I felt as a child; and how did I learn to deal with these things as a child? To run away and be by myself, or to go and look for someone else that I could feel better with.

There was one exception to this, although it ultimately happened for the same reasons: my maladaptive approach to relationships. I met this lady who after a few months, I found 'being intimate' with someone else. Now, it turned out that she did this because she was scared of how much she liked me and was prone to destroying things that were good in her life. I did try and give it another chance as I thought I loved her and could forgive her.

In my own way I did but was never able to completely let go after this and knew it wouldn't last. I did run away, to the other side of the world in fact! But I came back to endure what I ultimately knew was something that would never work. I think this is the biggest example of me trying to prove that despite everything, someone could want me. I know that she did as I could see it in her eyes whenever she looked at me, but I wouldn't allow myself to give to the relationship completely. However, she was the same and looked for the self-destruct button on many occasions due to the relationship she had with her mother. We were drawn to each other because of our patterns.

I went through a succession of meeting people who did treat me in a positive way, who would show me that they cared for me. I had no idea how to handle this and would do anything I could to sabotage it. I wouldn't treat them very well in the relationship, never making them a priority, and it wouldn't last very long as I rejected what I didn't know how to accept.

In one relationship, I even went clubbing with my friends and was standing next to the dance floor. My girlfriend at the time arrived with her friends and she came and stood next to me. With my whole being I wanted to turn to her and, well, just be nice to her, give her a kiss, show I wanted her there. But I didn't, I ignored her completely until she walked off. I felt terrible, but my subconscious was pushing her away, waiting for her to finish things so I could return to where I felt safe.

The way that I saw myself, felt about myself, and the way I thought others saw me and thought about me would influence and dictate my relationships for my first forty years. As I have reflected over the past during my personal journey of self-understanding and development, I can see many examples of how my self-perception was formed, influenced and reinforced, as my relationships with my family continued along the same themes, then my friendships and girlfriends followed similar and familiar patterns.

I had learnt how to 'do' relationships and learnt how to do them badly! OK, so maybe not badly, but very maladaptive and unhealthy for my own emotional wellbeing.

Whenever I entered a relationship I was always looking for an end result, and so I chose ones that would lead to this each time. What I mean by this is that my subconscious would seek out someone that eventually I would feel hurt by and generally unappreciated, like I wasn't enough for them. This would trigger the feeling that I would want to run away, I would look for someone else to appreciate me and eventually I would end up on my own, in my own space, in control of my own life, avoiding any pain, just as I did when I was a child. If they were nice to me in a relationship then I would ensure the same result, by getting them to walk away or switching off my emotions and finishing things when they got to a certain point where I started to feel scared.

Over the years I had formed a perception and opinion of myself and others that cemented and formed the basis of my deepest held personal beliefs – what I deserved and had an attraction to; what was 'comfortable'. When I say comfortable, it is what my brain had learnt to recognise as something I could deal with and manage, and although it would inevitably cause me pain, it knew I could survive each time.

Chapter Three
The Power of a Belief

I mentioned earlier that our brain's main function when we are born is survival and that is what I mean when I say that my brain had learnt to survive the pain I was experiencing. When I was looking for relationships in my life, I was looking for ones that I recognised. Ones that would be familiar to those I had experienced growing up and knew how to live with. In essence I was looking for relationships that would inevitably end in a certain way. By doing this I kept myself 'safe'.

I have come to describe this way of relating as 'Spikey' versus 'Cotton Wool'.

What I was doing in my life was 'Spikey'. I was attracted to relationships or situations (as this has also played out in other areas of my later life, such as my athletics career and work), that I knew would end with me feeling pain, like walking into some spikes, running away or then looking for something else. It would hurt, but I knew I could survive it.

When anything 'Cotton Wool' would arrive, something soft, loving and positive that could offer me the security that I was craving, I had no idea what this felt like so my brain told me to stay safe by avoiding it: like a survival instinct.

Now if something feels unknown or uncomfortable, I must check in with myself and give it a go before I dismiss it immediately as I need to prove to myself that I can survive it, and it may in fact be very good for me. If I am instantly attracted to someone in a certain way I need to seriously consider whether my subconscious is in play again, and my old attraction system has been triggered to something that would lead to a painful ending.

The 'Spikey' and 'Cotton Wool' thought process is born out of one of my belief systems: that it was better for me to go with what felt familiar, even if that would lead to pain, and to avoid what I didn't know something could lead to.

What is a belief? Well succinctly, it is something that we have experienced enough in life, or told enough to believe it to be true, but it is not a fact.

I use this analogy with my clients: If I was to spend your life telling you that a grey chair was red, you would believe that chair to be red if you have no other frame of reference. If someone then told you that the chair was grey, you would take a while to be convinced of this, and every time you saw the grey chair, you would likely see it as red and then remind yourself that it is in fact grey. The belief it is red has stuck and you need to challenge this every time, until you have a new belief.

So, what happens in our lives as children, that is then repeated in the same or similar circumstances, and we cannot rationalise it for what it really is, becomes a belief. If you were to think about your own childhood, if there were things that happened that caused you pain, did your parents take you aside and say something like: "I am really sorry that I have been unable to show that I really love you, or give you the time that you need to feel loved. My mum didn't really show me she loved me either and now I find it really hard to be close to people. I do love you and you are awesome, and you are not doing anything wrong"?

No, of course they didn't, because if they did I would doubt you would be reading this book at all. When those things happen in our lives as children, whatever that experience may be, we interpret it in our own way. If it is negative, then what we usually say to ourselves is "what have I done for this to be happening?" because as children we don't have the real answers and we will self-reflect to find those answers. It has to be about us and what we are doing as this is the only thing that makes sense; and then we try and modify our behaviour to change it, make it stop, or just cope with it (create a coping strategy).

This will lead us to relating in certain ways to fulfil certain needs that weren't fulfilled as a child. We will try anything to get the result we feel we need.

Why is a belief so powerful?

When we hold a belief, it becomes part of the way we live, and it can also be the only thing that can be more powerful than our need or will to survive. When I worked as a counsellor and talked with clients who wanted to harm or kill themselves, they saw it as the only way out of the situation they were in. They believed there was no other answer to their problems. We have seen on the news many times that people kill their families and then themselves as they believe that is the only option to stop the situation that they are in. They are driven by this belief for their pain to end.

When we are born, and even now as you read this, your brain is keeping you alive. It has a hardwired survival instinct and is programmed to do what it can to give you life. You may have heard of the 'fight or flight' response, also known as the 'stress response'. This is your brain's natural instinctive reaction to perceived danger. It wants you to be best prepared to either fight for life or run for your life and lots of instant reactions take place in your body, triggered by the brain to make this happen. This is where the feeling of fear comes from. It is there to keep you alive.

If you are prepared to die because of a belief, you are overriding your brain's primary function to live. That is immensely powerful.

Why are childhood beliefs so powerful?

As I have mentioned previously, when we are born our brain wants to keep us alive. It is negatively biased (why we always remember and feel negative experiences more than positive ones), so it learns how to be prepared for negative experiences when they happen again in our lives. If these things happen enough we form a pathway in our brain to deal with these situations, so when something happens that has happened before, our brain fires a message that it recognises this and has a way of dealing with it. It may be completely irrelevant to the situation we are in, but it is familiar enough for our brain to act in the same way.

Secondly, when we are children our brain waves are in the Theta state. These are much slower brain waves than in adults as we are in a phase in our lives when we need to learn and absorb a lot of information. The slower brain waves enable learning to be absorbed much more easily.

Imagine if you will that there is a child who experiences a lot of criticism from their parents, or who even perceives (and we will look at perception later on), that they receive criticism. It could be that they don't receive praise rather than are actually criticised or are only praised by one parent and are criticised by the other (remember that our brains are negatively biased). Their belief could therefore become one that 'I am never good enough'. Their emotions from this must be managed, so the brain develops a coping mechanism when this neural pathway is ignited and every time that this thought comes to mind, it is so deeply entrenched because it has been learnt while their brain is in Theta waves learning mode! Then if this belief never changes throughout their lives, how successful and happy do you think that this child will grow to be?

Next, imagine if they hold onto several negative beliefs about themselves, and how this may affect their life.

The last point about beliefs is the need for your brain to have them confirmed and constantly reaffirmed.

Have you ever tried to change something in your life that has been really hard to do? I know I have had several experiences when I knew that something I was doing had to stop and I was unable to do so, or I needed to see something through, but for some inexplicable reason I didn't.

This has been because I was fighting to dispel a deeply held belief about myself and it could likely be why you haven't been able to change things too. A belief is always looking for evidence to show that what you believe is true. If that is like my earlier example 'I am never good enough', then when we try and change something that goes against this belief, it fights back. This is what I call resistance to change when with my clients. We know we want to do something different, to make a positive change, but we won't because it goes against what we believe about ourselves. Our belief says "you don't actually believe this new stuff yet do you? So just come back to what you do believe" and then it actively seeks out evidence to reaffirm itself again.

That is the power of a belief!

Chapter Four
Good Luck Changing Others

Now that might sound a little derogatory at first read, but it is meant with the best of intentions.

Have you ever been in a relationship with someone and they had habits that you wanted them to change? How did they react? Were they eager and willing to try to change? I would guess probably not, and in some cases, the habit got worse, or the person retreated, and it just made your relationship worse.

There are lots of things I could go into detail with you about now that would explain why this is even happening and the subconscious processes that led to this point, but I will explore more about this when I get into the P.E.O.P.L.E. Programme explanation itself.

When I first went into therapy, there were so many things playing out in my background that it took me some time to get a handle on it all and this continued throughout my journey into personal understanding and development. One of the reasons why I have put my own coaching programmes together is to help people more quickly reach the point I am at, with fewer obstacles to overcome. But the thing I tried to do with my relationships was to get people to change who they were and what they did in order for me to feel better.

I will say that some people are a lot more amenable to change than others and that was really helpful to me; however, there were times when I was so frustrated and angry because people just wouldn't get it! They would stick to their stories and their way of seeing things and were unable or unwilling, or both, to help me with how I thought and felt.

An example of this was trying to get through to my father.

When I was around thirteen years of age I was very, very unhappy. I was in constant trouble at school and would do anything I could not to be there. I was suffering with debilitating migraines and very dry skin on my head, which I now know was caused by stress, and felt so alone in my life. My trouble at school was all around me feeling badly treated, that I could never do anything right and I wanted attention. I was going through the 'any attention is good attention' phase of my life. I had been consistently given detentions and excluded from school for a week when I was twelve for something I was really ashamed of.

There was a girl in my class at school who had a major crush on me. She would walk my way home from school, well out of her way and even wrote to the problem pages of a magazine to get some advice on how to get me to go out with her. I found this quite embarrassing and it became a topic of conversation in the class that everyone then would make jokes about.

I started to reject her for liking me and the negative attention I was getting. The anger built up inside until one day I lashed out and hit her; probably the worst thing I have ever done in my life.

At this time I was also really struggling with my home environment, which for me was quite toxic. I think that the thoughts and emotions of being unloved and unimportant there had really caught up with me and I just didn't want to be around anymore.

One night at home we were all sitting around watching television and my brother had done something to annoy me, again. I have no idea what that was now, but I remember it being the final straw for me at that time. My dad started shouting at me instead of him and I said that I wanted to leave the house and go and live with my mum.

Now, I didn't know my dad very well as I grew up as he wasn't around much and when he was he didn't really have any time for me. I have no memories of him ever playing with me or taking the time to see how I was and how my life was going. The only thing I ever got from him was negative attention when I had done something he saw as wrong. He was very good at showing his anger and disappointment towards me. Tonight, however was going to be the night that topped all of that.

As I screamed I wanted to leave home and go and live with my mum, it wasn't fair that everyone took my brother's side and I had had enough of being there, from what I recall he very calmly said "well, if you really want to leave, then go and pack your bags and I will take you to your mums." Being as upset as I was I went to my room and got a bag and started to pack some things to take with me. My dad then walked into my bedroom and said, "if you really want to go there is something I have to do first and you have had this coming for a long time." He then proceeded to rip all of my posters from the bedroom wall and screw them up, throwing them on the floor. Obviously upset I started crying and asking him to stop. He then grabbed hold of me, and for what seemed like an eternity started hitting me, and my memory of that now is, I really thought he wasn't going to stop and was going to kill me.

But he stopped, eventually, and left me in my room crying and went back downstairs. I don't remember what he said exactly at that point, but it was something like "you are going nowhere, and you can stay here until you are ready to come and apologise".

Me apologise! Me? For what? Now as you can imagine I didn't voice that as I knew what would come back at me, but I was so confused. What had I done to deserve this, except from expressing how I felt? How can this be my fault, again?

Sometime after this I did go to him and apologise, and this is probably the biggest example in my life where I have had to make things okay again because of the fear of the consequences if I didn't. I had some idea now what lengths he would go to to keep things the way he wanted them.

When I explored this many years later, it was suggested to me by my therapist that I address this with him, as it was something that had left me feeling traumatised: I really wanted an apology from him and to see that he knew he had behaved unfairly and was remorseful. I wanted some closure and to address the fact that I could not be wrong in this case.

How this fits into the idea that you cannot change others is because when I did drum up the courage to speak to him about it (which took me a while as my father really hadn't changed much over the twenty something years since it happened) I was unsure of what would happen. I was very surprised at his reaction though: he denied that it ever took place, at all.

In fact, I was shocked. Not only was there no apology, no opportunity for me to get the chance I needed to say how wrong this was, but there was a flat denial that it had happened in the first place. How was I supposed to deal with that? That showed me that there are people who will never change, never admit their responsibility in things and for whatever reason they do that, I cannot expect them to do so to make me feel better. I had to, and still do to this day, allow them to be who they are, for whatever reasons they are like it and manage how I am within myself instead.

I make a choice on how I am and how I feel with certain people, so that I can be the best I can be within myself.

I first asked my father about this incident around twelve years ago and have not revisited it since. I know I will still be disappointed if he gives me the same response but accept that he has his reasons for doing so and have made a choice to be okay with that.

I had to change within me for that to happen, and in this case, it was the only choice I had if it were to feel manageable.

Everyone has their reasons for being who they are, and if they are unwilling or unable to address these or maybe even unaware that these exist, then the only thing we can do is change ourselves to make it as right as it can be for us.

Through my work and understanding how people are and why they do what they do, I can see what my parents' issues probably are. I know they have struggled with their own 'emotional demons' that they carry since their childhood. This is why they have related to me in the way that they have. Some of this behaviour I will not condone, as it has been far too unreasonable and unwarranted, but I do understand them and their why, and that means I can manage it as I want to and feel about it as I choose.

If you are in a relationship where you are constantly waiting for a partner to change, or doing things to try and get them to, why are you there in the first place, and what does this say about your choices about who you have relationships with? Is it time that you accept that they can't or won't be changed and that you need to change within yourself to feel the best that you can feel?

What is the message you are telling yourself you deserve? What outcomes are you seeking to fulfil? What patterns have you established that reflect your beliefs about relationships and you when in them?

Chapter Five
Developing Relationships

I have already written about how my early relationships impacted on me, how my perception of them led me to believe certain things about myself and how I related to myself and others because of this.

By the time I was in secondary school, I had already made up my mind that female attention made me feel better about myself and I had chased this since the age of seven.

There is one incident that I experienced in secondary school that I think highlighted how I related to girls and would typify my relationships with them for many years to follow. It is an example of a relationship that cemented my beliefs and started the patterns of relating that continued into my early forties. It was also my first experience of what I know now to be emotional abuse.

At secondary school I wasn't well known amongst my peers until the most popular girl in the school saw me at a youth club one evening and then suddenly, I became the most talked about boy in my year group. Nearly every boy in the year had a crush on her and the other girls knew who she was. When she came into school the following day asking about me, the next thing I knew dozens of people were telling me she had a crush on me and wanted to know all about me.

Imagine the boost to my ego at that time! How could she have a crush on me? I just didn't know what to do with all the attention, but I remember that it made me feel good. I won't go into the details of the relationship or mention any names, but for a few weeks of my thirteenth year I was the talk of the school and lots of female attention then followed.

During the brief relationship with Miss Popular, I think I developed my 'go to' style with women as I did everything I could to be with her and make her happy, and she constantly abused my good nature and didn't treat me very well at all. This is the first relationship I remember chasing to get someone to be with me and the tears, anger and pain I experienced became a familiar pattern for me. To experience what I felt by being wanted by someone so popular, and then to be treated in such a way and then 'dumped' (as we called it in my school days) was heartbreaking for me. The frustration and anger I felt as a by-product of my pain was also very destructive in future relationships.

As I mentioned, I chased this positive 'I am wanted' feeling with her and then subsequent women, even when there was someone much better for me to be with I would chase what was bad for me and what I couldn't have. This girl being interested in me made me very popular with lots of girls; suddenly I was known and recognised. I dated a few lovely girls thereafter, but I always wanted to be wanted by her again and revisited the pain with her on several occasions, ending other, better relationships to re-kindle it.

After a year or so of this continuing, I don't know how or why but it stopped, and I moved on. Every 'nice' girl I dated thereafter, I would walk away quite quickly from, but if they were horrible or didn't really want me, something inside of me would pursue them - like I needed to prove to myself I was worth something if I got them. Then if I did I would want something else and chase that.

I had become attracted to the pain and increased my belief that relationships were painful and happiness temporary, just like with my parents.

The first really serious relationship I had was very much like the one I experienced in school. When I was 19 years old I met an older woman and after about six months I ended up leaving home to live with her. I knew it was a mistake before I moved in as I remember sitting on a dark hillside in Wales (after I left school I would go away on outdoor pursuit weekends based in south Wales to help out), telling myself that I knew that this relationship was bad for me and that I hoped she would finish it before we moved in together. Why didn't I finish it instead? Looking back now, it was because I felt like she needed me; I knew she loved me and I couldn't let that go, but I could walk away if she finished it.

This ended up being the most emotionally abusive relationship that I have experienced. The number of times I would end up in tears, feeling terrible about myself, that I wasn't good enough for her... I lost count.

I did try and leave several times, but she would threaten to kill herself if I did. In the end however the emotional abuse also turned physical and that is when I finally found it in me to say enough was enough and left. I could see the destruction it would lead to for both of us if I stayed any longer.

Would you believe that even after I had moved out and been away several months I asked her to take me back? Yes, I can believe it too, as my sabotaging neediness to be loved had kicked in and I thought I wanted to be back with someone who, I thought, loved me. I thank her to this day for saying no!

When I look back on my life and the relationships that I have experienced, I always felt like I was chasing something, and I now know I was trying to prove to myself that I was worth something as I never developed self-love or self-care as a child; I needed external validation in order to feel good about myself and someone else to make me feel better. Having had several relationships in my life where I have dated lovely kind-hearted people who would have done anything for me, I didn't believe I deserved this and had no idea how to accept it, so I would move on to something painful and destructive to reinforce my patterns and beliefs.

Again, as I write this and recall my past, there have been so many times that I have been in a state of desperation to prove to myself I was worth loving, but because that love wasn't coming naturally I tried to force it to get that proof. If someone didn't want me then I would do my best to make them, all because I didn't care enough for myself. And then when they did, my job was done, and I could move on.

I met a girl in a pub one night at a New Year's Eve party. She was with her fiancé but kept looking at me across the bar. I managed to sneak a couple of conversations with her and at the end of the night gave her my number. I am going to guess that as you have read this far, you will understand why I did it!

She was showing me an interest but was with someone else. I felt good about myself that someone who was very good-looking, and with someone else would want anything to do with me and so I pursued it. As you may also have surmised, it was a disaster. I chased and chased her for months and months until she finally chose me. Then I switched off a bit. Then I found out she was still engaged, so I switched back on again. She continued to see both of us for some time and then I reached my point of not being able to continue with such an up and down situation, but it took me around eighteen months to finally walk away. She chased me after that, but I had shut down from her and didn't want anything to do with her. Again, we were clearly drawn to each other because of our own destructive relational natures.

How did I finally become aware of this pattern? Well, I had been in therapy for a couple of years in my mid-thirties and I had trained and qualified as a counsellor but was still going in and out of relationships. I was aware of my life story and the emotions I had as a result, but I hadn't changed how I was, how I felt or what I believed about myself.

I mentioned earlier that I didn't know how to accept good things from people and this was very evident when I completed my personal counselling. In the final session, I wanted to say thank you to my counsellor, having realised that she had been the only person in my life that had really been there for me, listened to me and understood me. I cried as I expressed my thanks for this experience and have thought since that it was because of just that; her being the only person who had ever truly been there for me.

Upon reflection, I have realised that my tears weren't because she was the only one who had been there – she was the only one I had let be there for me. I had allowed this person to care for me, learn about me and fully share in my thoughts and emotions and my life. I had always been the listener before as I never saw myself as being important enough to have someone there for me, and I didn't deserve to be heard or cared for.

I also realised that I'd found an environment where it was safe to do so, because counselling is a safe confidential environment where the time is yours to be heard and understood; but it was also going to end, with no attachments or long-term expectancy or commitment. At the end of it all, I just went back into my world and did what I did, believing and perceiving in exactly the same way as before about relationships.

So, my pattern continued. My awareness of my story has made me just that, aware. What I wasn't aware of was the need for me to change in order to gain that happiness and fulfilment in life that I could have. I still didn't care about myself and I still believed that I didn't deserve much, and I also held on subconsciously to my idea of what relationships were, who I had to be and what was safe and unsafe for me emotionally.

Chapter Six
Developing My Personality

Imagine if you will, being aged eleven – you're the fastest sprinter in your school and you have been selected to compete at the district sports day. You may even have been that child yourself or were seen to be the best at something in your school. How did you handle the pressure and expectation?

The previous year I was certain I would win the district sports and came second. This year I really didn't want to go and compete in case I didn't win again. I wasn't sure if

I could really cope with it. People looked up to me being fastest in the school; the first time I had felt special or important, except for the attention of girls, in my life. How could I go and let everyone down?

"Miss, I can't go to the sports day today. I have fallen down the stairs and hurt my leg."

"Really John, how did you manage to do that?"

"I jumped down the stairs and fell and hurt my knee."

"Hmmm, are you sure that you have hurt yourself?"

"Yes Miss."

"Okay, you had better go and sit in class and I will go and tell someone that you will not be going today."

I knew that my teacher didn't believe me and I recall the mixed emotions of the embarrassment of lying to everyone and the relief that I didn't have to compete. That was tinged with the disappointment of my parents not even remembering I was supposed to be running at the district sports that day and asking how I got on later, but at least I didn't have to lie. I think the fact that my dad had come to watch the year before with my grandparents, and I hadn't won also affected my confidence and my decision on competing again. I wanted them to be proud of me and didn't want to tell them if I hadn't won again.

When training for my hypnotherapy diploma I revisited this event under hypnosis to explore whether this has anything to do with my sabotaging my athletics career and something else came up that I hadn't recognised at the time but made perfect sense when I realised it. At the same time as the district sports day we were working on group projects in class and it was the last day to work on them and finish them up. I had really enjoyed working on this project with my class mates and felt part of something, a belonging and I didn't want to miss out on finishing the project with them. This highlighted another need that I have struggled with since childhood, the need to belong, to connect and be part of something with others.

Back to my lack of confidence in my ability and living up to expectation. This stayed with me as I went to secondary school. As far as running was concerned, I wasn't the fastest child in my year when I went there. I was beaten on our sports day into second, and that didn't feel great, but I think it was also a relief as being the quickest and having to represent the school again was something I didn't want to face.

I didn't look again at the possibility of competing until I was fifteen when I joined Ilford Athletic Club with some friends, as I wanted to run the 800 metres. This was the time when Great Britain had excellent middle-distance runners, so again I think I was chasing some kind of kudos or wanted to be seen as something more than I was. As I was no longer the fastest in the sprints and was pretty good over the cross country we would run each year, I decided that I might be a good middle-distance runner.

Luckily for me, the youth team was short of a sprinter for the day I first went along to compete in their relay team, and so I was asked to step in. I won the 200 metres with a National Standard recognised time and so was asked to run the 100 metres too, where I also ran a National Standard time. Thank goodness for me that that happened. Not just because of what it led to, but it also meant I didn't have to do all of training for the 800 metres! That is hard, hard work.

When I returned to school, I then won our sports day and was asked to represent the school at the district sports once again. I said no at first as the old feelings came rushing back about how it might feel to lose.

A little aside story here. By this time in school, I had managed to completely turn my behaviour around and had even been made a prefect; I would then go on to become Head Student when in the Sixth Form. The reason for this was because I had a teacher at school that had sat me down the year before and taken the time to listen to me about how I felt, what was going on in my life and he told me that he could see so much promise in me, if only I was able to let myself reach my full potential (or words along those lines). I think he could see that I was in fact a very good kid trapped in a destructive pattern and that I deserved more for myself.

He included me in school trips that were just for selected children who he wanted to assist in living a different life. He could see who would benefit from just that little bit of value. He would talk to me about what was going on at home, the girlfriends I had, and always have a kind word to say and I always felt supported by him.

Even after I left school we still kept in touch and I helped out with other trips too at his request (the ones in Wales I mentioned earlier), making me feel valued and that I could also help others. I think this was also the first time I saw any value in myself and in helping people.

So, back to the district sports. I said no, that I didn't want to go, and this teacher took me aside and said, "you know that you won't be letting anyone down if you don't win, but you will be letting yourself down if you don't even try". I think I've remembered that advice throughout my life, because even though I struggled with my self-belief, I have always tried.

He even said he would come and support me, so I went to the district sports day, and I won!

Then I was selected to run for my district at the County trials, where if I won there I would be selected to run for the County at the English Schools Championships. Again, with his encouragement and support I went to the County trials, where I came second, but was still selected to compete for Essex at the English Schools, where I came sixth. That is when I decided that I had found something I could be really good at and competed in athletics for the next ten years or so. In that time, I got to a level of being an International Athlete and was selected for Great Britain at both Junior and Senior level. I won a silver medal at the European Junior Championships and a National Senior title.

All because one man had taken an interest in me and encouraged me.

What could we all achieve if we had the right support and encouragement in our lives, from someone who genuinely cared about us and wanted the best for us?

However, as I said, this did not change how I really thought and felt about myself at a deeper level and I sabotaged my athletic career whenever I knew I could do well at an event and there was a higher amount of expectation I placed upon myself. A good example would be in the most adverse of weather, gale force winds and rain, where there was no expectation of me running a good time, I would run a fantastic time for the conditions, but when I raced in perfect sprinting conditions, the expectation would get to me and I would run a similar time to that of terrible weather. Sometimes I would even get down into my blocks at the start of a race singing a song in my head. If only I had known then, how I was holding myself back from success and how to change my mindset to something positive.

The biggest example of how I held myself back from what could have been a great opportunity for me was when I was sent an application letter from a university in the United States offering me a scholarship. Now, I have no idea if I would have successfully got a place there, but due to me not really believing in myself and allowing this opportunity, I didn't even fill in the application, until I knew it would be too late to apply. The correspondence I received in return was that I had missed the deadline, so I may have got there if I had allowed myself to only try.

It took me fifteen years or so after I had stopped competing as an athlete to allow myself to look back happily and with pride at what I was able to achieve. My family have never talked about it, never saying how well I had done and I should be proud of myself. In fact, it has only been strangers that have remarked on how amazing it was that I had got so far, running for my country, that allowed me to start reflecting on the positives. Again, I think this is a sign of the people I chose to have close to me in my life, ones that reiterated it was never about me.

By the end of my teenage years, I think I had developed the underlying idea of who I was as a person. I held a deep sense of negativity about myself because of the relationships I had experienced as a child, and then those subsequently because of this, but I also knew that there was something positive about me that conflicted with this because of my teacher and his positive influence.

It is also interesting that the self-sabotage of allowing myself to have positive relationships in my life also affected that friendship, because as soon as my subconscious knew how to, I walked away from it and didn't go back despite how much I missed it at times.

I would like to take this opportunity to thank him for everything he did for me and how he helped shape me into the person I am today. I have no idea where I would be if it were not for his intervention.

Athletics was such a positive experience for me for so many reasons.

It proved to me that I was really good at something and I think that this was the main reason that I continued with it and proved to myself I could commit to something (although I will come back to this) as I was able to put the hours and hours of training in that was required to compete at such a high level. I had a reason to like myself and feel a sense of pride, even though I didn't really know how to accept it and, as I mentioned, it took me years to realise this.

That if my head was in the right place that I could aim for anything!

It gave me an outlet for my time and energy as my evenings and weekends were spent training and it kept me out of a world of trouble that was going on around me with other friends and family members. I am proud of myself that I chose this path instead of following the people that I was surrounded by in those other areas of my life.

I know now that I made a conscious decision to choose something more positive thereby walking away, and this also highlights my conflicted view of myself. I have known throughout my life that I am a good person as I have questioned so often why things turned out in a negative way, telling myself I didn't deserve it. My subconscious idea of myself however was completely at odds with what I deserved.

The people who I trained and socialised with throughout my athletics career were 'mostly' good role models, many of them older than me who encouraged me, believed in me and took time out of their lives to help me. Again, for that I am forever indebted. This again shows that I could make positive choices for myself.

A lot of the people that I knew growing up ended up in jail or were arrested for various reasons and I probably would have too had it not been for athletics.

Reflecting on what I now know about me, as I have got older I have found it very difficult to accept people doing something for me out of the goodness of their own hearts, especially when I couldn't even do something good for myself. I also realise that I had only allowed myself to commit so much to relationships before they triggered my fears of the past and I had to close down in order to protect myself.

Writing this now still brings a lump to my throat and an uncomfortable emotion to my chest as I think about accepting positives from people. I know that somewhere inside my subconscious I still have to fight the belief that I am not worth very much and I understand that I must keep doing this to keep myself from going back to my old belief systems.

Chapter Seven
So, What Changed?

Well, to be succinct and to end this chapter in one word. Me!

Chapter Eight... no not really, I will divulge my journey of change.

Counselling did have a very positive effect on me and from it I did feel better in general about life. There was a catharsis in talking things through and expressing how I felt. I knew the story about my life and the feelings around my relationships. And also, working as a counsellor for over a decade, I have seen the profound difference it can make to others. .

It changed me in some ways, but it didn't change my life, how I lived it or the relationships I had. I was aware of things but unaware of how to change them.

The big shift for me came when I met a leadership coach at an event I was attending. After a brief discussion they offered me an introductory session to see if coaching could help me. In that session we discussed some things that I was struggling with and they asked me questions that enabled me to see that I had this awareness of who I was, but I wasn't choosing to change anything as I thought I was stuck in my story forever. They allowed me to see things in a way I had never done so before and that I could decide the way I thought about them, and this would change how I felt about them.

The example was very simple. Being an athlete for many years, then trying my hand at bodybuilding and a brief dabble in rugby, I had learnt to see and define myself as and by being fit and looking in great shape, but that I must continue to train at the level I always had to sustain something within me. If I didn't exercise I would chastise myself, feel anger and frustration and then force myself to do something. The level I felt I must train at though was the same intensity as I always had, and after over twenty years at this level my body was telling me it was time to ease up. I didn't have to exhaust myself, feel sick and be generally wiped out afterwards, but if I didn't then I wouldn't feel okay: I needed to push myself to exhaustion to be content with the exercise I had done.

The coach enabled me to see that I was doing this because I had learnt to define myself by certain things and that if I was able to redefine this, by thinking differently and letting some things go, I could in fact be at ease with what I was doing and more importantly with who I was.

This tied into my past of being liked for looking fit and getting positive attention for it and it had created a perception I was struggling to maintain. In fact, I knew I didn't want to do this anymore but didn't know how to stop!

That ability to shift my thinking of how I defined myself and the emotional need that I was trying to fulfil gave me a sense of freedom and relief that I no longer had to do it anymore.

After a while of practising this new way and making shifts in other areas, is when I realised the impact of coaching and trained as a coach myself to be able to help others in the same way. There was an issue with this however, and it became a major issue; something else I was completely unaware of at the time that would cause me no end of trouble within myself.

I only allowed myself to change things so far before I would then resist the change, procrastinate and return to a place that made me unhappy and left me feeling unfulfilled.

As a counsellor and a coach, I had always been interested in hypnotherapy and decided to qualify as a hypnotherapist, to add to my repertoire of professional skills to help people, began a diploma course in hypnotherapy and psychology. What I now know is that this was all part of my self-sabotaging behaviour: as my counselling/coaching business was going well and I was in a good place, I felt I needed a change, to stop that success in its tracks rather than allow it to continue.

It is a decision that was led by subconscious self-sabotage and led me to understand the power of beliefs. Probably the most powerful thing that we will carry with us throughout our lives.

When I went to see Tony Robbins he told it something like this: We are born with a basic need to survive, and that is the primary function of our brain. It is built to learn and to keep you alive. A belief is the only thing powerful enough to overcome this. He uses terrorists as an example of this, that they are prepared to die because of a belief. I add to this the many clients I have worked with over the years who have had suicidal thoughts or have attempted to end their own lives, as they believe that this is the only way to end what they are going through. To them, and to you, I say there is always another choice.

While on my diploma course we looked at limiting beliefs and from a sheet with around one hundred of them on it, I could have ticked nearly all of them, I was able to figure out what my core belief was: that I would never amount to anything! This core belief was constantly looking to be fulfilled, and so I would do things and put myself in situations over and over again that made this belief real. Once it was fulfilled I felt 'safe' as I was back in the place that my subconscious was telling me I was comfortable with.

Challenging and changing your limiting and core beliefs will change your life. It completely changed mine and I have allowed positives into my life ever since. I allow myself to look forward without doubt, and believe that I can achieve if I put my mind to something; I accept good things and deserve them to happen.

I definitely wouldn't stand up in front of people and tell my story or make videos about coaching and the concepts of coaching that I have learnt and created, or even contemplate writing this book if I hadn't lived the life of change that I have over the past few years. It is a major step indeed that I have even called my coaching company John Kenny Coaching. I remember several times in the past when I have been asked my name, and by just saying John I have felt uncomfortable or even embarrassed. I thought it was because the name John was very popular as I grew up and was a common boring name. I now realise that for me to be so affected by just saying it was because I was embarrassed to be me; I rejected who I was at a very deep level.

Self-development and learning about who I am has changed my life. It is my passion to help people to feel this too. The benefits that they can achieve through my coaching have been amazing, to live a life that they choose, rather than the one that they think they should, expect to or have to will have freed them to fulfil their goals and dreams like they never realised they could.

The next part of this book is to talk about The P.E.O.P.L.E. Programme, what it is, how it came together and how it will help you.

Chapter Eight
The P.E.O.P.L.E Programme – Why?

I hope that from what you have read so far that you have already gained an understanding as to why I have written The P.E.O.P.L.E. Programme.

It was originally devised to help with your relationships by helping you to understand yourself and how you impact on the life that you live: what holds you back in relationships; how you relate to others and how they relate to you because of who you are, or what you allow to be seen. Also, to help you to understand others, as by being able to do this you can decide how you want to think and feel when around them. By having this scope of understanding about relationships you are able to choose who and how you are at any given time.

What I didn't anticipate at the time The P.E.O.P.L.E Programme was originally devised, is that by learning about and understanding you, it will create a confidence within you that will completely change your life and give you the ability to choose the direction that your life takes, in all areas.

It has inspired and affirmed the Interpersonal Relationship approach to coaching as the right way for me to help others, as I have helped myself. I have clients I work with who want weight management coaching, or career coaching and of course relationship coaching, and by using this approach they can address any issue in their lives that they are struggling with and stop hitting the same barriers again and again.

All of my clients have developed an awareness of self that leads to them being able to choose their own way forward and make decisions from a healthy place of belief, overcoming old belief systems as they arise. One thing I haven't mentioned so far, and I wish I could fit everything in detail into this book, is about our values and principles. If we are not living by these in our lives, then we will also struggle to be happy and fulfilled.

By looking at yourself you will learn what your values and principles are, where they come from, are they imposed or something that are really yours? Living to our own values and principles leads to a more fulfilled life and is extremely important to our overall happiness.

Our needs must be met. Our drivers are based on this happening and depending on what your needs are and where they come from will impact directly on your quality of life. My coaching approach will look at these in detail, where they are based, how they are met, or not, where they come from, are they yours and serving you positively?

Relationships, how important are they to your wellbeing?

Well, the seventy-five-year Grant and Glueck Studies about happiness carried out by Harvard Medical School and published in 2013 concluded that the main link to happiness in life was the quality of our relationships (I will point out that this study had only male participants, but do not think the results would have concluded any differently with other genders).

What makes for the quality of relationships that we have with others is the quality of the relationship that we have with ourselves, who we then allow to be in our lives and at what level, and then how we manage them.

And that is, in essence, why I have written The P.E.O.P.L.E. Programme.

To help you to improve the relationship that you have with yourself and therefore every other area of your life. By having a healthy relationship with you and being your most authentic self you will increase your self-belief, confidence and esteem. It will enable you to make choices based on what you really want for your life and leave or manage the things that you don't want in a different and positive way.

What do the initials of The P.E.O.P.L.E. Programme stand for?

Chapter Nine
The First P of The P.E.O.P.L.E. Programme

The first P of the programme starts at the beginning by looking at the **Problems** that you are having. We cannot even begin to understand what needs to change and find a solution unless we know what the problems are.

I like to say that "understanding leads to acceptance, and acceptance gives us the ability to move on".

To know what the real problems are, explore them and then really understand where they come from gives you the ability to do something about them.

I work with a lot of clients who have issues in their lives, knowing that they are doing certain things or that certain things are going on but they don't know why or what they are stemming from. When we explore these, we can get to the root cause of the problems and put things in place to change it/them.

When trying to understand what is really going on in your life, try asking yourself these questions.

What is affecting your life?
List the things that you know are causing a negative effect on you.

What impact do these problems have?
How do they affect your life, what situations do they lead to, what emotions do you feel and what are they leading to or stopping you from doing?

How long have they been an issue?
Can you put a time to when these began? By understanding the triggers to problems, we can look at the circumstances that caused them to arise in the first place and see why they are still present in your life today.

As you have read so far in this book, a lot of my issues were caused by belief systems that I established as a child and had been carrying for well over thirty years. Can you trace problems that began in your childhood that you haven't been aware of or found difficult to put behind you and move on from?

Are these problems things that affect all aspects of your life? Relationships. Career. Business.

Sometimes what affects one area of your life will impact on all of them. Struggling with a negative self-belief led me to sabotage all areas of my life just to prove to myself that it was true: my relationships, athletics career and business.

Where do they occur the most? When are they at their most powerful and influential on you?

Are you very capable in one area of your life and find that you struggle in others? Do you show that you can be your authentic self at work and focus and achieve your goals and dreams, but your relationships seem to cause you stress, insecurity or pain?

This then brings us to the four 'W's.

Who? What do you do? What do others do? Is it specific people or circumstances?

This is looking at who is involved with your problems. What type of people tend to bring these problems up the most – is there a specific type of person?

I tended to struggle around people that reminded me of my past and then I would revert back to how I managed those relationships as a child.

Do you recognise how these people are behaving, what they are saying or not saying that stops you from doing something positive?

When? At what times does it occur? In what situations? (What situations take you to a place that you find difficult and are there any similarities that you notice?)

What are the cross-over behaviours? (do you notice that you act or feel a certain way in more than one situation/ with more than one person, but the emotions are similar or the same?)

What? What is actually happening? What has been said/ done? What are the likely situations? What do you feel? What are you thinking?

Why? Probably the most important question of all. What are the beliefs and perceptions that you hold that lead to the issues in your life existing in the first place?

We have discussed the power of a belief and how we perceive things in our own mind and the impact that this can have on our thoughts and emotions.

In each of the chapters explaining The P.E.O.P.L.E. Programme I will add a brief case study to show a practical example of how it has been used with previous clients.

Case Study: Problems

I saw a client a while ago who came to see me as they were unable to cope on a daily basis with their relationships and with their business.

They were in a state of emotional overwhelm but didn't realise it at the time. They thought that they may have Attention Deficit Hyperactivity Disorder (ADHD) because they were unable to concentrate for even short periods and were having regular emotional outbursts.

After our initial session of going through where they were at in their life, what they thought and how they felt it became clear that they had a lot going on. They had lost a parent for whom they had not grieved, had fallen out with a close family member, and were under a lot of pressure to be a success in their business but were full of self-doubt.

By talking this through they were able to gain a clearer picture of what was going on for them, why it was happening and when it was triggered the most powerfully. The work could then begin, to manage, change and move on from where they were.

Chapter Ten

The First E of The P.E.O.P.L.E. Programme

As you may have figured out by the end of the previous chapter, the E stands for **emotions**.

The most important thing to know about emotions are that they drive everything that we do. Tony Robbins says that 'emotions create motion'. We act on how we feel, and emotions lead us to the life that we live. The underpinning concept behind Interpersonal Relationship Coaching is The Bicycle Affect and if you have watched the video I have made on this then you will know how our emotions directly influence our choices and how we react to situations in our life. If you haven't seen it, have a look on the John Kenny Coaching YouTube page to get a brief explanation.

If you feel something, whether positive or negative it is more than likely that you will act on whatever has caused this emotion. If you don't feel it, then you are likely to not care about it in the first place. We need to be aware if we genuinely don't have any feelings for something or if we are blocking out feelings to avoid something, such as overwhelm.

The questions to ask about your emotions are:

How do you feel? Sometimes these can be hard to understand and pin-point exactly, but that is likely because we don't ever take the time to really look at how we feel and understand our emotions.

Why do you feel this way? What do you think is happening that has caused them?

Where do these emotions come from? Another thing that we don't have a tendency to do is try and understand where in us these feelings arise. Where do you feel them in your body? What might be the connections that we are missing?

When did you first notice these types of emotions? Again, we need to look at how long we have felt this way to know how long we have carried them.

In what relationships/circumstances do they feel most powerful?

What is the complexity of the emotions that you feel? We can 'mix up' our emotions as we can feel more than one thing at a time or get confused by how we are really feeling.

Guilt is a good example of this as many people feel guilty when there is no need for them to. ***So if it isn't guilt, what is it?***

What emotions are you ultimately left with? Is this the real emotion or a result of something deeper?

When we look at what we are left with we can explore the reality of the situation that we have been in. As with the example of guilt we can explore the real emotions we are experiencing; worthiness, deservedness, shame and fear are examples of emotions that we could have that we mistake for guilt.

Emotions are incredibly complex sometimes but can also be very straightforward to understand. The more that you understand them the easier they are to contextualise and manage. They deserve to be given the time that you need in order to recognise them, process them and decide if they are relevant to the situation you are in, or come from another place in time, from another person or situation, and ultimately not real in that moment.

Case Study – Emotions

My client was finding it hard to motivate themselves and commit to their relationship. They felt angry, didn't want to do anything or go anywhere and had detached from their partner. They were convinced their relationship was over and were lost as to what to do moving forward.

So what emotions were they experiencing that led to them feeling this way. After some discussion they realised that they felt very angry about something their parents had done a few months before, and their partner kept reminding them of the event as they were very upset by it. What had been brought up was how their parents had treated them as a child, and it wasn't anger they felt the most, it was a sense of rejection by their parents, leading them to not feeling worthy of love. Because of this they had decided they were not worth loving and had stopped caring for themselves and would not let the love in from their partner, who was reiterating the thoughts by reminding them of what had happened. Once they realised how they really felt and why, they were able to process this, challenge it and create the emotion they wanted instead.

Chapter Eleven
The O of The P.E.O.P.L.E. Programme

Once we have looked at our problems and how our emotions influence our lives, we then look at how we **Operate** as a person. Recognising how you react and understanding why you react in certain ways will lead to you to gain the ability to choose how you want to be rather than feeling that you are compelled to do something because of how you feel. As mentioned, you react on your emotions and what we want to be able to do is respond to things instead.

A reaction is something instantaneous and comes from a subconscious part of your brain that compels you to act in a certain way. You can break this word down into re-(act), as in this is a reenactment of an event from your past. Your brain is warning that there is something going on that you don't like, and it goes into its database of experiences to tell you how to manage this, even though it may have no connection to the actual situation that you are in.

A response is something thought through and measured to the reality that you actually are in.

Do you really need to feel angry when someone doesn't do what you want them to do, or can you decide that a more appropriate emotion is more suited to that situation? Can you choose to be responsive rather than reactive?

When these situations arise, I have devised a series of questions that you can ask yourself to decide what you are feeling and why you are feeling this way. Once you have a clear picture of what is really going on, you can then tell yourself how you want to be instead of following what you think you should be.

The questions to ask yourself are:

1. *What do you do when you feel certain emotions?*
   How do you react? What is happening to your body?

2. *How are you within yourself? Are you still in the present moment?*
   Where are your thoughts? Have you gone off into your subconscious and your past and are re-living a similar feeling/situation from then? Is your brain telling you that

you should/have to do something right now as this is what it has learnt to keep you safe?

3. *How are you with others?*
   How do you see them? What are they trying to do 'to you'? Are you chasing them, or trying to escape from their presence? Do you need to hurt them to defend yourself?

4. *How do you see yourself?*
   What is the belief that you are re-living about you? What are you saying to yourself to back up these beliefs, what type of language are you directing at you?

5. *How are you being seen?*
   This will generally be related to how you are seeing and feeling about yourself. Your judgement of you is what you will believe others are seeing too.

6. *What does this behaviour lead to for you?*
   When we act in a certain way, we are looking for a specific response from the someone or the situation that satisfies our need in that moment.

Are there consequences that you know will occur if you do a certain thing? What result are you seeking from your behaviour, how do you think you are going to feel at the end of this? What will it have achieved for you? And, are these going to be positive or negative for you or those involved.

As we have achieved an outcome in the past from operating a certain way, it is now a pattern that we follow even if this may not serve us positively as our brain is just looking for a certain familiarity.

I use anger as an example here again as I have worked with anger a lot in the past. Not just from my own upbringing, but I also used to run the anger management courses for the NHS in north London when I worked there as a counsellor, and have written my own anger management courses.

Anger is never the first emotion that you feel; it is always a secondary emotion that is used to manage the primary one. We learn at some age that anger is how we manage a certain feeling that we otherwise do not know how to cope with.

Examples of how it is used in different ways:

Do you know someone who gets angry to get what they want? They can be shouting at you one moment and then smiling at you the next, sometimes in a 'smug' I have got what I want way, or in others it is as though nothing has happened. In this case they are using anger to gain an outcome, and once that outcome is achieved then there is no need to be angry any longer. Their emotion has been managed and they are quite happy to move on.

The real emotion however has not been addressed.

Other people may go quiet as they do not know how to manage how they feel so they react in the only way they know, and that is to shut down.

Case Study: **Operate**

I will use myself as the 'Operate' Case Study.

Let's go back to my story and how I felt as I grew up around rejection and not feeling as though I was wanted. When this feeling returned through my life, one way I would deal with this was to become desperate, trying to cling onto people who I thought were going to leave me.

This holding on would become physical as I couldn't cope with the expected pain of them not being there anymore. My reaction was completely over the top to avoid what I thought I would feel.

If they stayed (although they may never have come back again after that), I would quickly calm as my fear of that pain had been allayed.

What I learnt to do was respond to these situations. If I am now with someone who doesn't want to be with me for any reason, I do not take this as rejection. I realise that some people will want to be around me, and some people won't, so my response is always measured. I will sometimes ask if they are unhappy with something I have done, as they may well be. If required I will apologise for this and how they feel about it, but the emotion of desperation never comes up.

What are you or are they trying to achieve by how you operate?

How does this behaviour impact on the situation you are in?

Does it drive people away, or get them to do what you want?

What is the gain or loss at this time? (We will look at this more closely in the next chapter.)

How does it affect your relationships short and long term?

Knowing how you operate gives you an insight into what is really happening in that moment and at that time, so you can have a deeper understanding of what is really going on for you and the choice to choose a different behaviour that is going to be more beneficial to you in any given situation.

Chapter Twelve
The Second P of The P.E.O.P.L.E. Programme

Now, I find this part the most interesting and insightful and the game changer in a lot of the things that cause us the most negative outcomes in our lives: that is our **Patterns**.

Our pattern of behaviour is incredibly important as it shows us where we return to each time something happens in our lives, when we have reached a point that we don't know how to do it any differently.

Our pattern will not follow exactly the same path each time we encounter a situation, but it will aim to take us to the same or a similar result. This can work in a positive and negative way. If we know something works for us we can follow it to get a desired result, so knowing your patterns will give you a way to get to where you want to be, as your experience will show you how to achieve it.

I am going to tell you here about the craziest relationship that I have ever experienced, which summarises nearly all my negative patterns into one.

I was set up by a friend, to meet one of her friends who she thought would be a great match. Now, she didn't tell me this until it ended, but she set us up because she thought that I would be good for this person, who had been in some very traumatising relationships and lost her mum in her teens. She said it was about time she had someone nice in her life.

As you are probably already aware, we both came into this relationship with issues. Mine were being worked on as I had been a therapist for about a year at this point. But I wasn't aware of my pattern. I was instantly attracted to her and we dated for a few months. Everything was going okay, I will say okay, as with hindsight, there were some major red flags.

It came to my birthday and we had got dressed for the evening. I paid her the usual compliments about how she looked, but on this occasion something in me wanted it to be reciprocated. I had done my usual, being as nice to her as possible to win her over and had reached the stage of wanting something in return.

Let me just say that when I asked she hardly spoke to me for the rest of the day! Until she got drunk that evening and then let go of whatever had been triggered in her by me asking for her to say something nice. I don't think I did it in an appropriate way with the 'what about me' line, but after that day she backed right off, and I chased her. She wouldn't call for days or tell me what she was doing, she would call me when drunk to say she loved me and missed me and then not talk to me, and I didn't let it go. In fact, it was Christmas soon after and I showered her with presents to prove how much I cared and how much she needed to like and appreciate me.

She then didn't speak to me for several days. I hung there like a trooper until she agreed to meet me for lunch. During lunch we agreed to try again from the beginning and spent the rest of the day together. We then went to a club and had some drinks. When I went off to the toilet, she disappeared! I finally managed to reach her about an hour later and she had gone home. When I got there, she went hysterical telling me I had to leave and even called the police to say I was harassing her and wouldn't leave her flat.

I sobered up and drove home, after sitting in my car freezing for a while. The next day she called me around twenty times. When I finally decided to answer she asked why I had gone home and said that she hadn't done anything wrong and that I had overreacted!

My final words to her were, never call me again and go and get yourself some therapy!

As you can see, yet another example of me hanging on in there with something very destructive just to try and prove to myself that I could be loved and accepted. It took the extreme outcome to get me to realise I needed to walk away.

Let us now look at how these elements fit into The P.E.O.P.L.E. Programme and how we go about recognising our pattern in our relationships, and again I will use myself in the 'Patterns' Case Study.

Case Study: **Patterns**

As you read earlier in the book, I experienced a series of events as I grew up that taught me about relationships. During those experiences I made a decision of how relationships worked and acted on those throughout my life.

I learnt that relationships were unstable, untrustworthy and would always end in me enduring some pain that would lead to a certain result.

Those results were:

I would feel some kind of rejection that would lead me to do one of three things. Not that I necessarily do all three every time, but they were my 'go-tos' when I was young.

1. *As a child, when I felt rejected at home I would run away, just to see if anyone cared about me enough to come and find me or stop me from doing so.*

2. *I would go and look for friends to play with outside where I could feel part of something, cared about and that someone wanted me around.*

3. *I would play on my own in my room with my toys.*

As I grew up I would choose relationships that followed this pattern as I couldn't trust in them and I didn't know another way of relating. I had an expectancy of how relationships would turn out and

I already had that planned out in my mind when I chose partners and friends.

What this looked like was: Firstly, I would meet someone new, and my subconscious would work out if they reminded me of how relationships worked. If they did, my brain would feel 'safe' in embarking on some kind of relationship with them and I would engage, already knowing in my mind the end result.

If they didn't trigger what I recognised, then that relationship would go no further as I did not know where it would lead to. There were a few exceptions to this, when I met some people that were good for my life, but I always found a way to get things to end the same.

Secondly, after a while of me trying to show them that I was the best thing since sliced bread and giving all I thought I could give, I would then start to back off as I wanted to know if they would then chase me if I started to run away.

Thirdly, I would then go and look for someone else to play with. As I had nearly always chosen someone who wouldn't chase me, or who couldn't be there for me, I needed to find someone who then paid me the interest that I was craving again.

Lastly, I would end up on my own. This is where I felt the most content and safest, being by myself where no one would be able to reject me. But this was also where I was at my most sad, feeling sorry for myself, like 'look, this has happened to me again', not realising it was me making it happen.

The other interesting part here is that, all of the people that were choosing to have relationships with me, if they hadn't worked on their issues before, were choosing me to fulfil their relationship pattern too. My subconscious was attracted to their subconscious, and oh what a disaster of a subconscious relationship we would embark upon!

So, when we look at our subconscious patterns, we can also look at other people's too. This will give us an insight into what they need and why they are choosing the relationships they do, and what we are triggering in them as well as ourselves.

A few quick questions to ask yourself when it comes to patterns are:

What are my triggers? What are you looking for as an end result, really! Not what you are saying you want from a relationship.

I used to say I wanted to be loved and appreciated. Well, yes, I did, but I wasn't really looking for that. I was looking for a way to feel safe, to be on my own.

What do you trigger in others? What might their pattern be, that your pattern connects to?

What routine do you follow? Do you notice in yourself similar feelings from the past? What are you re-creating by entering this relationship?

What do you want others to follow? What reaction are you looking for?

What result is it you are trying to achieve? Is there a perceived safety in returning to this way of being again and again?

If you take the time to sit and think and to figure this out, you will never have to follow the pattern again if you choose not to. You can create a different outcome, the one that you truly want for your life.

There is a quote by Carl Bard that says "although we cannot make a brand new start, we can start now and make a brand new ending!"

Chapter Thirteen
The L of The P.E.O.P.L.E. Programme

When all becomes clear about how your life has been and how your experiences have shaped your perceptions and beliefs, what do you see is the **Likelihood** of your future?

How do you see the issues in your life now that you have a clearer perspective on them? Knowing that you are the author of your own life and everything that is happening is based on the internal stories that you tell yourself, what can you tell yourself right now?

How do you see your life if these things continue the way that they are, if you don't change anything?

Continuously difficult relationships?

Unable to improve the relationships that you have?

Not being able to let positive things into your life?

Continuing to feel the hurt and pain of the past every time that something comes up that triggers you?

If someone had asked me before I met the coach who got me to look at things differently, I would have said that, this is my story, this is how it is, and this is how it is going to be, how can I possibly change my life! Well...

I needed to change how I allowed my story to affect me. I needed to change my beliefs and how I perceived myself in my life in order for me to make the necessary changes. And most importantly of all, I needed it to be something that I wanted above all else. The motivation to change cannot exist unless it is more powerful than the motivation to stay the same. The emotions that you want to feel must outweigh those that keep you the same.

So, how would you like to feel?

Imagine a life that you want, where you can feel as you want at any given moment and decide how you are going to respond to events that happen, as they happen. To be able to make plans and set goals and allow yourself to fulfil your potential and live your dreams!

What kind of relationships could you experience? The new ones you could have and the ones that already exist.

What does that feel like? Is that a better feeling than what you currently experience? Is that enough for you to make the changes you could make?

By the way. It isn't easy. Have you heard that anything that you need to change within yourself is the most difficult thing that you will ever do. It is a twenty-four-seven exercise to begin with as we look to overturn all the years our brain has got used to 'helping us survive' in the best way it knew how. It needs to learn to let go – to know another way isn't going to kill us – and embrace change.

And let me tell you something from my heart to yours: it is well worth the effort!

Case Study – Likelihood

I worked with a client a few years ago who had a very difficult upbringing. They were left with a relative when newly born, and up until the age of five lived with a family friend who they thought was their mother. When they were five their father appeared and took them to live with the rest of the family. They had no idea who this person was, they never got to say a real goodbye to their 'mother' and no one explained what was happening.

When they arrived at their new home they weren't wanted by their siblings or their real mother, only their father, and after a while of being bullied and ignored they were sent to live with someone else. A couple of years later they were taken back to their family again, but were again bullied, and felt unwanted, except by their father.

During this time, they would try and fit in and do anything and everything for anyone to feel wanted and part of the family, but they never did. When they were old enough, they left the family home and never returned.

As they got older, they attracted the same types of relationships over and over, where they would give a lot and receive very little until they had enough and left. They even said to me in one session about the current relationship that they were in: If someone offers me ten per cent, it is better than the two per cent I got as I grew up.

It is interesting that our coaching would stop and start as they couldn't cope for very long with the thoughts and emotions that came from change. After several sessions they would start to feel better and put things in place that meant they could change their idea of relationships, but would then stop the sessions or just not engage in them, and go back to being in their 'safe space'.

A while later they would return and try again, but disengage again after several sessions.

When they returned the third time they had finally decided that to continue as they were was untenable, as it was too painful, and were able to finally address their life and choose a new way forward, living, not just surviving, where they could choose who they had in their life for the positives they could bring, and achieve their goals and dreams because they were finally going to let themselves do so. If they hadn't done so, the likelihood would be that they would have always felt the same and experienced difficult relationships, over and over.

Chapter Fourteen
The Second E of The P.E.O.P.L.E. Programme

I will keep this final part brief as we have more or less covered it all in the previous chapters. In fact, we have covered it all in the previous chapters, so this is where we **Enhance** our lives by putting it all together.

When I work through the programme with my clients, this is where we look at how we consolidate everything. Your story and how it came to be, how it led you to see things a certain way and how it instilled in you a belief system that constantly needed to be reinforced.

We look at the relationships that you have in your life, the one that you have with yourself and how this has changed as we have worked through the programme together.

The most common thing to come across at this stage of the programme, as the changes start to take shape and my clients are about to go it alone, is resistance (see previous case study).

Remember that pesky brain of yours and its need to keep you safe. Those belief systems that you hold that look to be reinforced at every opportunity. Well, this is generally when they go to war with you as you try and change your life to the one that you truly desire. But that is okay, as we have ways of dealing with those and it is a war that they cannot win.

They may get a few victories as they will get us when we are down, tired, struggling with illness, when something negative happens in our lives and sometimes when we just don't seem to be able to recognise or manage the triggers. But... they will never win the war to change as we have so many ways to overcome them and move on swiftly when they appear.

So, what is your future going to look like? What is the likelihood of you living the life you choose, making it as fulfilling as it can be, feeling an inner confidence within you to take on any task, set any goal, allow any relationship and live your dreams?

I am sure you will understand how this will work if we look at each section, as we can see how it is all put together to get the result that you are looking to achieve.

As this is the whole six parts put together it would not be a brief case study, so I will condense it as much as I can.

Case Study – Enhance

I shall begin at the beginning with the very first client who went through these steps in their coaching sessions with me and give you a brief outline of where they are now, as they do touch base every so often to update me on this.

They came because they were depressed, were finding it hard to function on a daily basis and were using alcohol to cope. They had been advised by their partner to seek help or the relationship was over.

So, what were the problems?

The main issue was that they could only focus on how negative things had been in their life and could only see a negative future. They were constantly worrying about how things would turn out and feeling upset about how things had been.

The deep underlying issue was how they felt about themselves because of their past, how they saw themselves in the present and what they anticipated they would become. They had never felt loved or cared for by their parents and were constantly run down by them and believed that they were worthless. The relationships that they then experienced, partners and friends, cemented this feeling as no one was ever there for them, but partly of their own doing as they didn't allow it because of how they felt about themselves, undeserving of good things. Their partner also fed this idea by constantly putting them down, with nothing ever seeming to be good enough for them.

An aside here. I often come across clients who can do ninety-nine good things , but the hundredth is all that their partner, parents and friends remember or comment on. If this is something that happens in your life, then those people will never be able to appreciate what you do and it's maybe time to stop trying! It is not you!

The emotions that my client experienced were ones of rejection, sadness, worthlessness and asking themselves 'Why me'? Or being a victim of their life. The constant focus of their problems and experiencing these emotions led them to feel depressed and lacking in any motivation.

Not knowing how to change their behaviour, they operated by trying to keep everyone happy and proving themselves to others to gain external acceptance. They would change who they were to fit who they thought someone wanted them to be, losing more of themselves as this continued. This only exacerbated the issue as they were never really accepted anyway and felt like they were nothing to most people. They managed these feelings of overwhelm by drinking in order to numb their thoughts and not feel anything as often as possible, as it was too much to cope with.

Their pattern, as previously noted was one of keeping themselves stuck in relationships where they constantly sought approval, but as they were expecting to be rejected they only sought approval from those who couldn't give it to them and reaffirmed their belief they couldn't be loved, and all relationships would end the same.

This was also only half the truth, however, as my client chose not to notice those in their life who were not like this. They had some friends who could be there for them, and had been there for them, but as this didn't fit into their belief system or what they allowed in their lives, these friends were completely discarded from their thoughts.

The likelihood was clear. If this continued their life would be one of misery and hopelessness, and this is all they could see.

It took them the full six months of the programme, plus a couple of add-on sessions to fully turn this around. By implementing the changes that they wanted to make in how they saw themselves, who they allowed in their life, what thoughts they chose to have and the emotions they could then experience, they were able to stop drinking, improve their personal relationships and those at work (they did split from their partner after a while as they gave them every opportunity to accept the real them, but they were unable to do so).

Now, they have set up their own business, one they had always wanted to do but didn't believe in themselves enough, have a new and happy relationship, have good friends that they allow to be there for them as much as they are in return, and have accepted their parents for who they are and manage those relationships on their own terms, making sure that their old triggers are not fired as before.

Chapter Fifteen
Not Just Relationships

There are so many great things about getting to understand yourself.

All of the things that I have talked about in this book around relationships, and how by getting to know yourself gives you the ability to change how your relationships will be from now, on is amazing in itself.

If you look at the brief history of my life journey from the first few chapters of this book, you can see that I learnt to perceive things in a certain way based on the experiences that I had, the circumstances I was involved with leading to some maladaptive belief systems embedding themselves in my brain.

This in turn caused my brain to react in certain ways to situations that triggered my past and what I had learnt, and to seek certain ways to fulfil my relational needs based on what I thought relationships were supposed to be like, in order to keep me in a safe, known space.

There are a lot of things to take from my story, but the most important one is that no matter where you have come from – no matter what kind of background, family or schooling you had, whether you were financially well off, taught to learn and then get a job, mortgage, settle down and have a family – if you take the time to really understand yourself, who you are, where you come from, what you think and feel about you, relationships or even just life, you can choose to be whoever you want and become whatever you put your mind to, if you know how it is working for you, positively and negatively.

I have been able to release the hold on me my beliefs had, the negative influences of family and friends, and decide what life I want to live, the people that I want in it and let myself be the most successful I can possibly be.

Another and very important thing that I have found I experience because of the work I have done on myself is – and according to Brendon Burchard is a fundamental need in being able to live a great life, to which, since I have felt this way I completely agree – to feel free! Freedom from my past, freedom from my subconscious thoughts and beliefs, freedom to choose how I feel at any given moment, is, well, just plain freeing, and dare I use my over-the-top American word here... Awesome!

Epilogue

So, there you have it.

My life of relationships nicely wrapped up into a few thousand words.

My journey to find out who I really am and realise all that I can be.

But... this journey will never end, not until I have taken my last breath, I would presume. Every so often I discover something about myself that I need to think about. Even after all the work I have done on understanding myself, I still slip into old ways where my subconscious is choosing my path for me. The great thing about that is that I now realise it before it goes too far, before I get myself into a position where I need to run away, find someone or something else and end up on my own feeling 'safe'.

In fact, I would not have let my wife into my life if I hadn't checked in with my 'scared' self when we met. After a couple of dates, I very nearly told her that it was going nowhere and that I didn't want to continue seeing her. Before I actually made that mistake I had a major word with myself as to why I felt this way. Yes, my old way of relating had appeared. There didn't seem to be an out for me, there didn't seem to be pain ahead, there were no tell-tale signs that I would end up on my own once again. This led to the unknown and my subconscious wanted out! Only when did I challenge this did I allow myself to make a different decision, to tell myself it was ok and what would be would be and I would be alright whatever happened, I would be okay and why not give this a go and see where it ends.

A couple of weeks before I got married I met someone new on a professional level, and when I met her I was instantly attracted to something about her. Again, I needed to have a swift chat with my subconscious to see what this was all about. I immediately realised that she had all the traits of someone who I would have had relationships with previously, that my destructive pattern had emerged. I was able to turn this 'off' straight away and the feelings disappeared as soon as they had arrived.

This is an ever-evolving journey that I watch as it happens. I am aware that there is still a part of me that is a child in immense emotional pain, as he surfaces every once in a while, to remind me of what I went through, and even kicks off when I least expect him to, as something in my present is being triggered from my past. But I am there for him/me now, to offer him/me all the love and support he/I have ever needed, and, by changing who I have in my life, they can offer him/me something too, that tells him/me that life is good, and it is all going to be okay.

And it is my wish that you will be able to do the same.

Much love

John

Perception:

The Oxford English Dictionary describes perception as:

1. *The ability to see, hear, or become aware of something through the senses.*

2. *The way in which something is regarded, understood or interpreted.*

The reason I add this is to point out that it doesn't matter what actually happened in your life that led you to think or feel a certain way. What matters is the way that you perceive it and the meaning you give to it based on your perception.

Some of the things I have written about in this book people will disagree with as they have their own memory of it and their own perception of that event. This is how I remember it and this is how I have been affected.

I could watch a movie with you and at some points you will laugh, and I may not, or I will cry, and you wouldn't know why. This is down to the meaning that we give things, based on our perception of our experiences.

This is important to remember as this is the only thing that matters when it comes to your personal recall and your emotions. You are **not** wrong in how you remember things.

What is equally important to remember is that you can change how you feel by changing the meanings that you give if you need to move on from something that is holding you back.

I am John Kenny, the UK's Leading Interpersonal Relationship Coach and have been helping people from around the globe to live the best lives possible for just over a decade (at the time of this publication).

I have written my own positive mindset, stress management and anger management programmes and of course The. P.E.O.P.L.E. Programme. The Bicycle Affect is the key concept behind my coaching methodology and is available to watch on my YouTube Channel as well as being available as an eBook.

I hope that you have very much enjoyed reading about these parts of my life and that you can relate to and take support from aspects which can help you work through the things that you need to in order to live the healthiest relationships that you possibly can, and especially the one that you have with yourself.

Thank you to everyone who has helped me in my life, with special thanks to:

Mr William D Patterson for seeing something in me as a teenager that no one else took the time to help me find, and for your friendship.

To Diane and Gary – knowing that I can rely on you has meant the world to me at times when I felt alone.

To Lorren – for making it easy for me to love someone.

To my parents – I know that I may have given you a bad rep in this book, but I appreciate everything that you have done for me in my life, for the times that you have been there and for the person that I have become. I know that you have had your own struggles in life and you did and do the very best you can for me.

Lightning Source UK Ltd.
Milton Keynes UK
UKHW020321240119
336107UK00005B/104/P